MAGNETISM

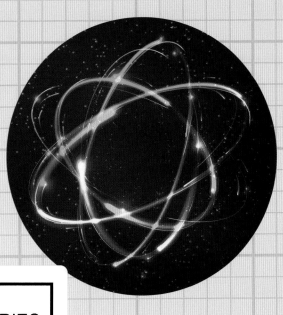

Louise Spilsbury

raintree
a Capstone company — publishers for children

Raintree is an imprint of Capstone Global Library Limited, a company incorporated in England and Wales having its registered office at 264 Banbury Road, Oxford OX2 7DY – Registered company number: 6695582

www.raintree.co.uk
myorders@raintree.co.uk

Produced for Raintree by Calcium
Edited by Sarah Eason and Amanda Learmonth
Designed by Simon Borrough
Picture research by Susannah Jayes
Production by Victoria Fitzgerald
Originated by Capstone Global Library Ltd © 2016
Printed and bound in China

ISBN 978 1 4747 3110 2
20 19 18 17 16
10 9 8 7 6 5 4 3 2 1

British Library Cataloguing in Publication Data
A full catalogue record for this book is available from the British Library

Acknowledgements
We would like to thank the following for permission to reproduce photographs: Shutterstock: ArtisticPhoto 30–31, Art of Sun 1, 8, Cozyta 12–13, Daisy Daisy 40–41, Gustavo Fadel 45t, Aleksandra Gigowska 17r, Arto Hakola 24–25, Pat Hastings 14–15, Imagesbyruthwilson 4, Imageman 34–35, Jordache 16–17, Manfredxy 29br, Matt9122 25tr, MilanB 6–7, 20–21, 21tr, Robert Neumann 34b, Nevodka 36–37, Pi-Lens 22–23, Snowbelle 22b, Solarseven 44–45, Takasu 9, TFoxFoto 28–29, Vaclav Volrab 30b, Wlad74 5, Worradirek 13b.

Cover art reproduced with permission of: Shutterstock: Denkcreative, Lineartestpilot.

Every effort has been made to contact copyright holders of material reproduced in this book. Any omissions will be rectified in subsequent printings if notice is given to the publisher.

All the internet addresses (URLs) given in this book were valid at the time of going to press. However, due to the dynamic nature of the internet, some addresses may have changed, or sites may have changed or ceased to exist since publication. While the author and publisher regret any inconvenience this may cause readers, no responsibility for any such changes can be accepted by either the author or the publisher.

Contents

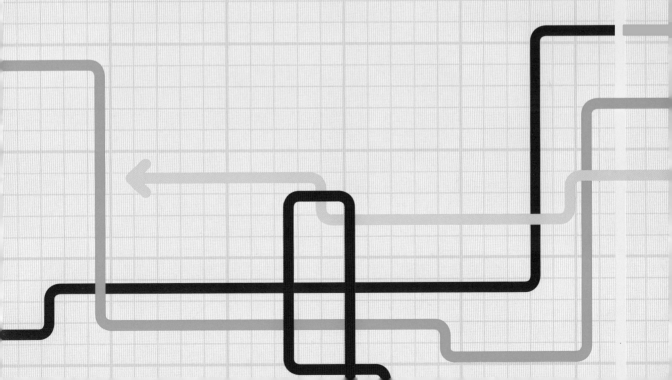

Chapter 1
What is magnetism?

Magnetism is an amazing and mysterious type of force. A **magnet** is an object or material that exerts a magnetic force. A magnet can attract, or pull, certain types of metal materials and objects towards it. It can also repel, or push, those metals away. What is special about magnetism is that it is a force that can act on other objects without even touching them. There are many different kinds of magnets but they can all exert this amazing power!

These plastic letters are attached to small, thick, rectangular magnets so they can stick to a refrigerator door.

There are magnets in many of the things we use every day, without knowing they are there. Magnetic clasps keep purses and camera cases closed. Magnetic strips stop cabinet doors from swinging open. Magnets are also used to produce electricity, and without them our computers, phones and other machines would not work. **Motors** use magnets to make them work, so there are magnets in most machines that have moving parts, such as fans, food mixers and electric toothbrushes.

Forces that are used to push or pull objects must usually touch the material they are moving. When you want to pull a book towards you across a table, you make physical contact with it. Magnetism is a non-contact force. A magnetic material does not need to touch an object to apply its power. Magnets produce a magnetic force that can be applied through air, water and even some solid materials, such as paper and plastic.

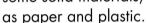

A lodestone is a naturally magnetic piece of a mineral called magnetite. Magnetite contains iron.

Get smart!

Historians believe that the ancient Greeks and early Chinese civilizations knew about magnetism. They each discovered a special, rare type of stone, called a lodestone, which had the power to attract iron. The word "magnetism" probably comes from an area called Magnesia in the country that is now Turkey, where ancient civilizations found many of these magnetic stones in the ground.

Magnet poles

One magnet can be used to apply two different forces: it can be used to repel magnetic objects or it can be used to attract them. How can this happen? The secret lies in a magnet's two ends, or **poles**.

The opposite ends of a magnet are called the poles. One end is the magnetic north pole; the other is the magnetic south pole. The magnetic force produced by a magnet is strongest near its poles. Different, or unlike, poles attract each other. If you place the south pole of one magnet near the north pole of another magnet, they will pull together. Like poles repel each other. So, if you place the south pole of one magnet near the south pole of another magnet, they push apart. Magnetic earrings stay on because of magnetism. Each of the earring's two parts contains a small magnet. When two opposite poles of the magnets face one other, they pull the two parts of the earring together through the ear lobe to hold the earring on the ear.

Some magnets are stronger than others, but all magnets can only work over a certain distance. The strength of the magnetic force from the poles of a magnet becomes weaker the further you move from the magnet. Other materials can also block the magnetism. For example, the two magnets that pull together to close a purse will only work when the opposite poles are very close together. They will no longer attract each other if something comes between them. Magnetic forces can work through many materials, but they pass more easily through some than others.

Horseshoe, or U-shaped, magnets like this have the poles side by side. The blue end of a magnet is usually the south pole. The red end of a magnet is usually the north pole.

How magnets work

Magnetism is an invisible force caused by the movement of tiny particles, called **electrons**, that are invisible to the human eye. These tiny particles carry electric charges inside **atoms**.

Atoms are the building blocks of all matter. There are more than 100 different types of atoms in existence, and they combine in different ways to form every substance in the universe. We cannot see atoms, but scientists have discovered that an atom is made up of a central **core** of matter called the **nucleus**, which contains **protons** and **neutrons**. Electrons **orbit** the nucleus in a similar way to how planets orbit around the Sun in space. Electrons follow an almost circular path around the nucleus, and each electron spins around and around at the same time at incredible speeds.

This simple diagram of an atom shows the path taken by electrons as they orbit the nucleus.

As the electrons move, they create an **electric current**. This makes each electron work like a very small magnet. Electrons in most atoms exist in pairs, with each electron spinning in an opposite direction. This means that the magnetic effect of one electron in a pair cancels out the effect of the other. Atoms in paper have equal pairs of electrons, which is why such materials are only very weakly magnetic. However, some metals, including iron, have atoms in which electrons are not working in pairs. When these unpaired electrons spin in the same direction in an atom, they can line up with each other and make the atom magnetic. When all the atoms in a substance create magnetic forces that pull or push in one direction, the substance becomes strongly magnetic.

This magnet contains iron, a metal in which all the atoms create magnetic forces that pull strongly and attract the metal paper clips.

Get flowchart smart!

Why magnets are magnetic

Follow the flowchart to see why magnets are magnetic.

In the atoms that make up all matter, electrons orbit the nucleus.

Electrons moving in pairs in opposite directions cancel out the electric charge each creates.

Together, the atoms create a strong pulling force, which makes the material magnetic.

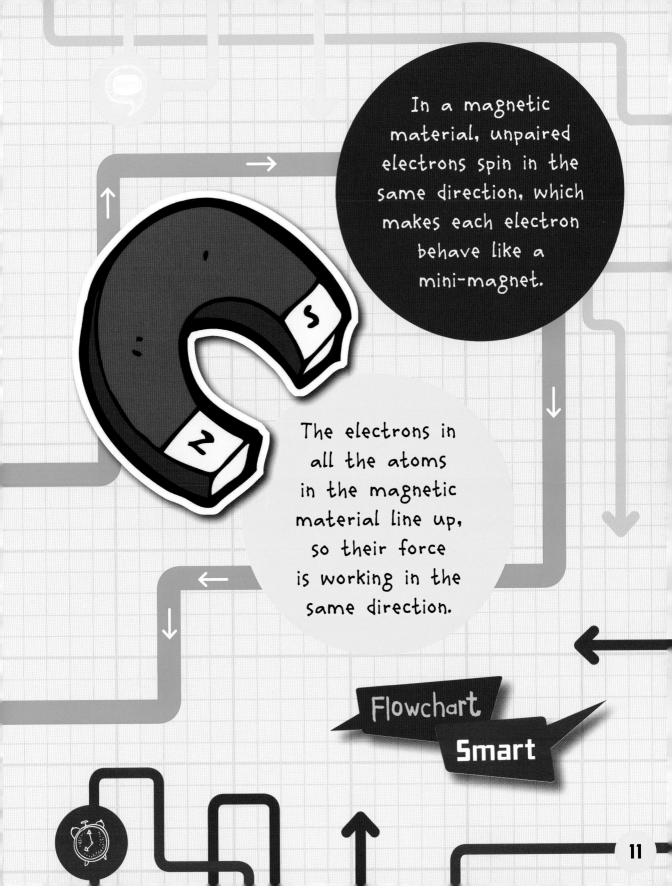

In a magnetic material, unpaired electrons spin in the same direction, which makes each electron behave like a mini-magnet.

The electrons in all the atoms in the magnetic material line up, so their force is working in the same direction.

Flowchart
Smart

Chapter 2

Magnetic materials

Magnets attract other magnets, but they can also attract materials that are magnetic. This is how a magnet can stick to a refrigerator door. All magnetic materials are metals, but only a few metals are magnetic.

Iron is the most common magnetic material, and any metal that contains iron will be attracted to a magnet. Materials such as iron that are strongly attracted by a magnetic force are said to be **ferromagnetic**. Steel is also a ferromagnetic material, because it is an **alloy** containing iron and other metals. Most other metals, such as copper, aluminium, brass, tin, silver and gold, are only weakly magnetic. That is why a steel food or drink can is attracted to a magnet, but aluminium cans are not attracted to a magnet. Recycling centres use magnets to sort out steel cans for recycling into steel, and aluminium cans for recycling into aluminium. You may see a magnet symbol printed on some steel cans.

In addition to iron, other ferromagnetic materials include nickel, cobalt and some alloys of rare earth metals such as the silver-white gadolinium. These magnetic materials can become **permanent magnets** and retain their magnetism for a long time. For example, steel is made from a mixture of metals, and this makes steel harder than iron and causes it to keep its magnetic properties longer than iron alone.

Not all cans are magnetic. Drinks cans are made of aluminium and will not be attracted to a magnet.

An alnico magnet is a powerful permanent-magnet alloy that contains iron, nickel, aluminium and one or more of the elements cobalt, copper and titanium. Alnico alloys have a high resistance to loss of magnetism, so they stay magnetic for a long time.

This giant magnet is being used to separate, lift and move magnetic metals quickly and easily.

Temporary magnets

There are two basic kinds of magnets: permanent magnets and **temporary magnets**. It is possible to make a new magnet by exposing a ferromagnetic metal, such as iron or nickel, to magnetic forces. When the newly magnetized metal is heated to a high temperature, it becomes a permanent magnet. Permanent magnets are harder to make into magnets than temporary magnets, but they are more useful because they keep their magnetism longer. Temporary magnets are made from materials that are easy to magnetize, but that lose their magnetism quickly and easily.

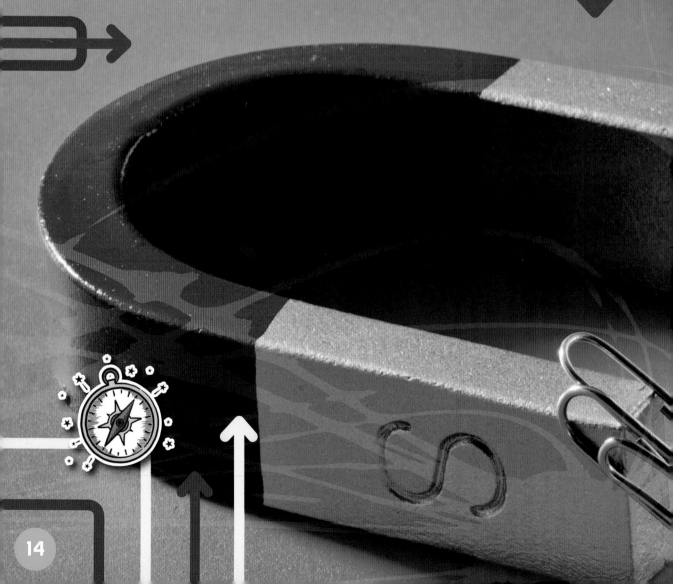

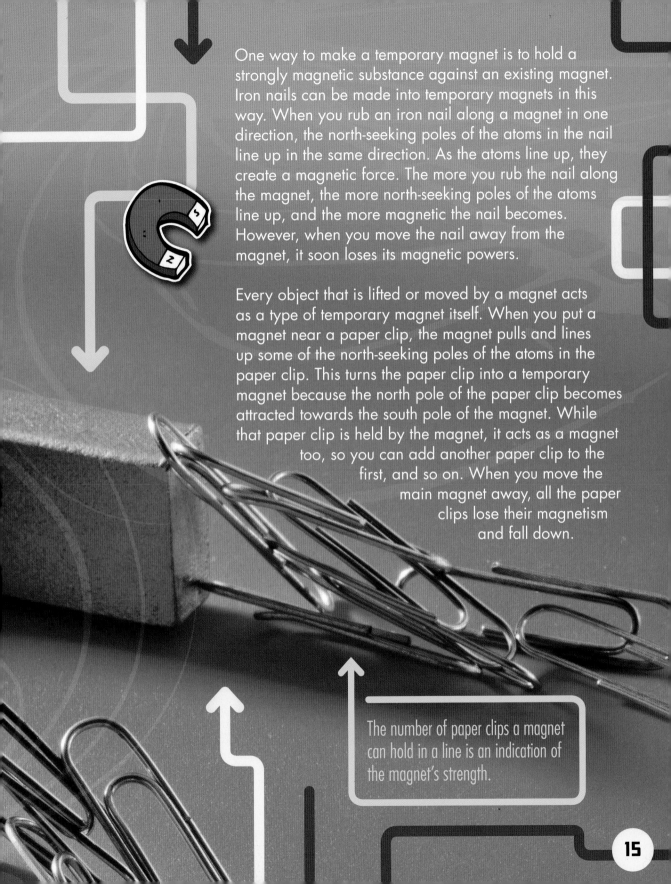

One way to make a temporary magnet is to hold a strongly magnetic substance against an existing magnet. Iron nails can be made into temporary magnets in this way. When you rub an iron nail along a magnet in one direction, the north-seeking poles of the atoms in the nail line up in the same direction. As the atoms line up, they create a magnetic force. The more you rub the nail along the magnet, the more north-seeking poles of the atoms line up, and the more magnetic the nail becomes. However, when you move the nail away from the magnet, it soon loses its magnetic powers.

Every object that is lifted or moved by a magnet acts as a type of temporary magnet itself. When you put a magnet near a paper clip, the magnet pulls and lines up some of the north-seeking poles of the atoms in the paper clip. This turns the paper clip into a temporary magnet because the north pole of the paper clip becomes attracted towards the south pole of the magnet. While that paper clip is held by the magnet, it acts as a magnet too, so you can add another paper clip to the first, and so on. When you move the main magnet away, all the paper clips lose their magnetism and fall down.

The number of paper clips a magnet can hold in a line is an indication of the magnet's strength.

Losing magnetism

Temporary magnets lose their magnetism easily, but permanent magnets can lose their magnetism, too. There are ways to prevent permanent magnets from losing their magnetism.

Ferromagnetic materials, such as nickel and steel, lose their magnetism if they are heated to a high temperature. Heat causes the electrons in their atoms to become too agitated to stay pointing in one direction for long. Magnetic materials lose their magnetism at different temperatures. Nickel loses it at around 350 degrees Celsius (660 degrees Fahrenheit), while iron must be heated above 770 degrees Celsius (1,300 degrees Fahrenheit). Some of the strongest magnets are stored in cool places when not in use to stop them from losing their magnetism. A magnet can also become **demagnetized** if another magnet moves across it in different directions, or if it is knocked or dropped.

This steel is so hot it is glowing. Nickel, steel and other ferromagnetic materials lose their magnetism if they are heated to very high temperatures.

The magnetism of permanent magnets follows a path between the poles. If the path is made more difficult, for example if the magnetism has to travel through a gap or other non-magnetic material, it can lose some of its strength. A horseshoe magnet has a gap between its two poles, and if it is stored as it is, it will slowly lose its power. To prevent this, an iron bar called a **keeper** closes the gap. The keeper forms a loop through which the magnetic forces pass, and stops the magnet from losing its magnetic power.

If the magnetic strip on a credit card becomes demagnetized, the credit card will no longer work.

Get smart!

When shops swipe a credit or debit card, the black magnetic strip on the back of the card gives them all the information they need. If two cards are stored so that their magnetic strips are facing each other, the magnetic strips can become demagnetized.

Get flowchart smart!

How magnet keepers work

Follow the steps in this flowchart to understand how magnet keepers do their job.

Bar magnets are stored in boxes in pairs.

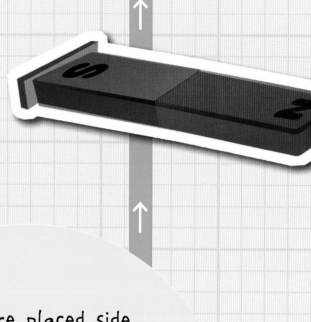

They are placed side by side with unlike poles opposite one another, so the north pole of one magnet is next to the south pole of another. This stops them from constantly repelling each other and weakening their magnetism.

Soft iron bars called keepers are placed across the ends.

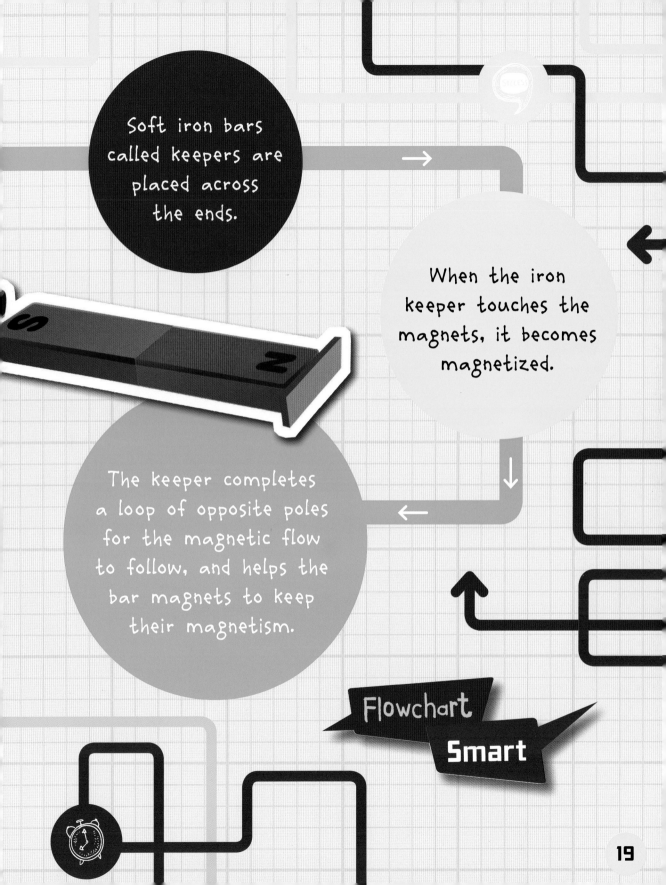

When the iron keeper touches the magnets, it becomes magnetized.

The keeper completes a loop of opposite poles for the magnetic flow to follow, and helps the bar magnets to keep their magnetism.

Flowchart Smart

Chapter 3

Magnetic fields

Magnetism is a force that can act across a distance. Its power can be felt in a three-dimensional zone around the magnet. This is called the **magnetic field**, and every magnet is surrounded by one. We cannot see the magnet's magnetic field, but we can see the effect that it has on other magnetic materials.

Every magnet produces a magnetic field that is stronger around its two poles. That's why the iron filings being pulled towards the magnets in this picture are clustered together at the ends of the magnets. The iron filings form lines around the magnet known as magnetic field lines.

Get smart!

A magnet of any size always produces a magnetic field with two poles. If you slice up a magnet, you simply get a smaller magnet with two opposite poles. You do not get one magnet with only a south pole and one magnet with only a north pole. The only thing that changes is the strength of the magnets. The two smaller magnets will not be as strong as the bigger single magnet.

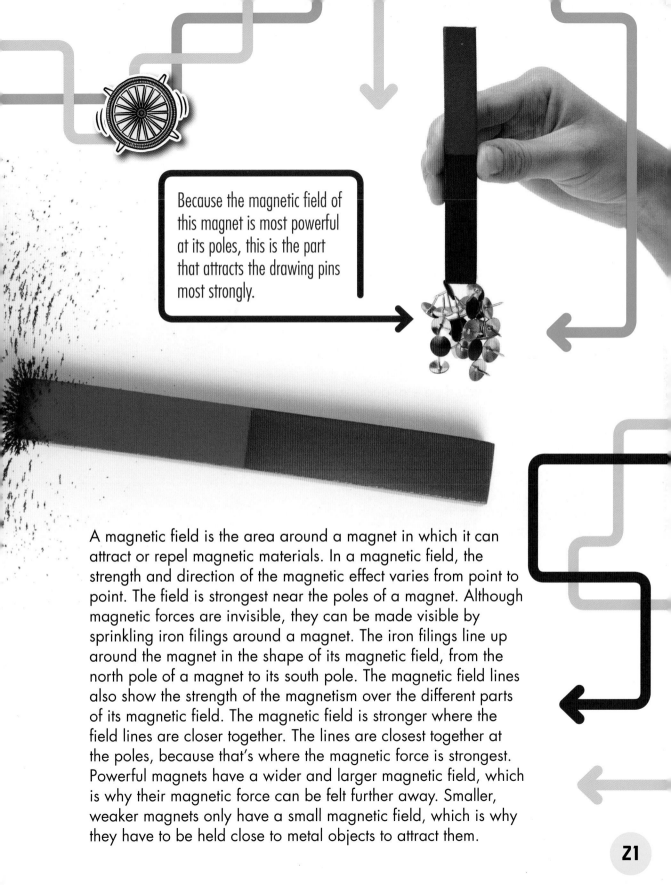

Because the magnetic field of this magnet is most powerful at its poles, this is the part that attracts the drawing pins most strongly.

A magnetic field is the area around a magnet in which it can attract or repel magnetic materials. In a magnetic field, the strength and direction of the magnetic effect varies from point to point. The field is strongest near the poles of a magnet. Although magnetic forces are invisible, they can be made visible by sprinkling iron filings around a magnet. The iron filings line up around the magnet in the shape of its magnetic field, from the north pole of a magnet to its south pole. The magnetic field lines also show the strength of the magnetism over the different parts of its magnetic field. The magnetic field is stronger where the field lines are closer together. The lines are closest together at the poles, because that's where the magnetic force is strongest. Powerful magnets have a wider and larger magnetic field, which is why their magnetic force can be felt further away. Smaller, weaker magnets only have a small magnetic field, which is why they have to be held close to metal objects to attract them.

Earth's magnetic field

Did you know that Earth is a magnet? Our planet's core contains iron and nickel at temperatures so hot that some of it is in a constantly melted state. Scientists believe that rotation in the spinning liquid of the outer core creates electrical currents that produce Earth's magnetic field. Approximately every 200,000 to 5 million years, Earth's magnetic field switches positions. The north pole becomes the south pole, and the south pole becomes the north pole.

Earth is so large, and its magnetic core is buried so deep within it, that by the time its magnetic force reaches the surface its magnetism is far weaker.

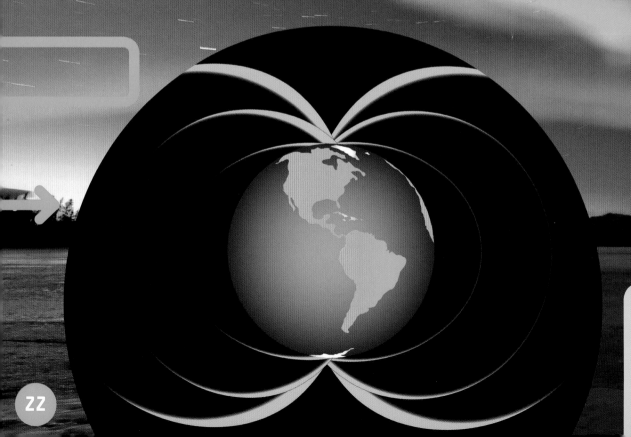

Earth's magnetic field is so big that it stretches into space. It is called the magnetosphere. The force from the magnetosphere acts like a shield and protects Earth by repelling harmful rays from the Sun and particles that would destroy the atmosphere if they entered it. Earth's magnetic field has field lines similar to those found around a bar magnet, just much, much bigger. The magnetic north and south poles of Earth are the places where the planet's field lines come together. Unlike the points on a map that we call the North and South Pole, the magnetic north and south poles keep moving. Although the magnetic north pole is now very close to the point on Earth we call the geographic North Pole, not long ago it was in Arctic Canada!

The *aurora borealis* is seen here over northern Canada at dawn, as particles from the Sun collide with Earth's atmosphere.

Get smart!

Near Earth's magnetic poles, it is often possible to see amazing displays of glowing, multicoloured light patterns in the sky. Around the magnetic north pole these displays are called the *aurora borealis*, and around the magnetic south pole they are called the *aurora australis*. These incredible effects are created by Earth's magnetic field. They happen when tiny particles from the Sun pass through the magnetosphere and interact with substances in the atmosphere as they follow Earth's magnetic field lines.

Using Earth's magnetic field

Earth's magnetic field is very useful. Humans and animals around the world use Earth's magnetic field to **navigate**, or find their way around, and plan which route they want to take. **Compasses** containing magnets are some of the oldest navigational tools in history. They have been used by people for hundreds of years and are still in use today.

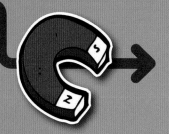

A compass contains a small magnetic needle that sits on a **pivot**. The needle can spin freely in all directions. The compass needle responds to Earth's magnetism so that its needle always points to Earth's magnetic north, near the North Pole. It is important that the magnetic needle is lightweight and spins easily or it will not move easily enough to always point north. Earth's magnetic field is weak at the surface because the magnetic force has a long way to travel from the centre of the planet. Thick, heavy compass needles would be unable to respond to this relatively weak force.

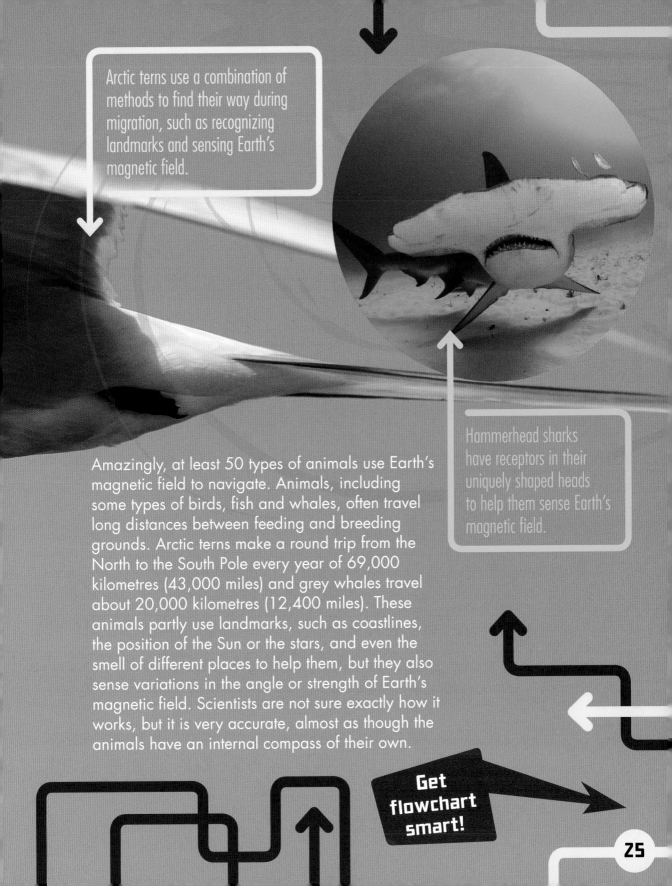

Arctic terns use a combination of methods to find their way during migration, such as recognizing landmarks and sensing Earth's magnetic field.

Hammerhead sharks have receptors in their uniquely shaped heads to help them sense Earth's magnetic field.

Amazingly, at least 50 types of animals use Earth's magnetic field to navigate. Animals, including some types of birds, fish and whales, often travel long distances between feeding and breeding grounds. Arctic terns make a round trip from the North to the South Pole every year of 69,000 kilometres (43,000 miles) and grey whales travel about 20,000 kilometres (12,400 miles). These animals partly use landmarks, such as coastlines, the position of the Sun or the stars, and even the smell of different places to help them, but they also sense variations in the angle or strength of Earth's magnetic field. Scientists are not sure exactly how it works, but it is very accurate, almost as though the animals have an internal compass of their own.

Get flowchart smart!

How a compass works

Let's take a closer look at how compasses work using a flowchart.

A compass is placed on a flat surface.

The magnetic needle inside the compass responds to Earth's magnetic field.

The north end of the compass needle always points north, so you can rotate the compass until the "North" marking aligns with the needle. The other markings on the compass show you where east, south and west are.

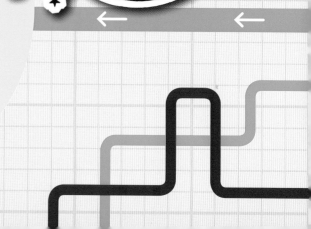

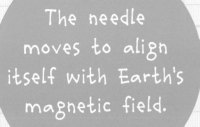

The needle moves to align itself with Earth's magnetic field.

The north end of the compass needle magnet points to the magnetic north pole, which is roughly the same as our geographic North Pole.

The south end of the compass needle magnet points to the magnetic south pole, which is roughly the same as our geographic South Pole.

Flowchart Smart

Chapter 4

Electromagnetism

Electromagnets are a special and very useful type of magnet. In an electromagnet, a magnetic field is generated only when electricity flows through it.

Electricity is the flow of moving electrons. When electrons move, or hop, between different atoms within a substance, they carry electrical **energy** from one place to another. When electricity runs through a wire, it generates a magnetic field around that wire. If you wind the wire around a ferromagnetic metal such as iron, the magnetic field of the loops of wire increases the effect of the magnetic field. The metal becomes magnetized and turns into an electromagnet, with the strength of the magnetic field produced by the electric current coming from the coils of wire. To make a more powerful magnetic field, you can wind the wire into tighter coils around the metal, or increase the electric current flowing through the coil. This creates an electromagnet that is stronger than normal permanent magnets of the same size.

Electromagnets are very useful. Permanent magnets always produce the same strength of magnetic force. Electromagnets are different. They are only magnetic while an electric current is flowing through them. Once the electric current stops flowing, they are no longer magnetic. This means electromagnets can be turned on and off at the flick of a switch. Electromagnets are used in places such as scrapyards and recycling centres. When the electromagnet is switched on, it can attract, lift and hold metals while a crane moves them. When the electromagnet is turned off, it drops the metals in a new location.

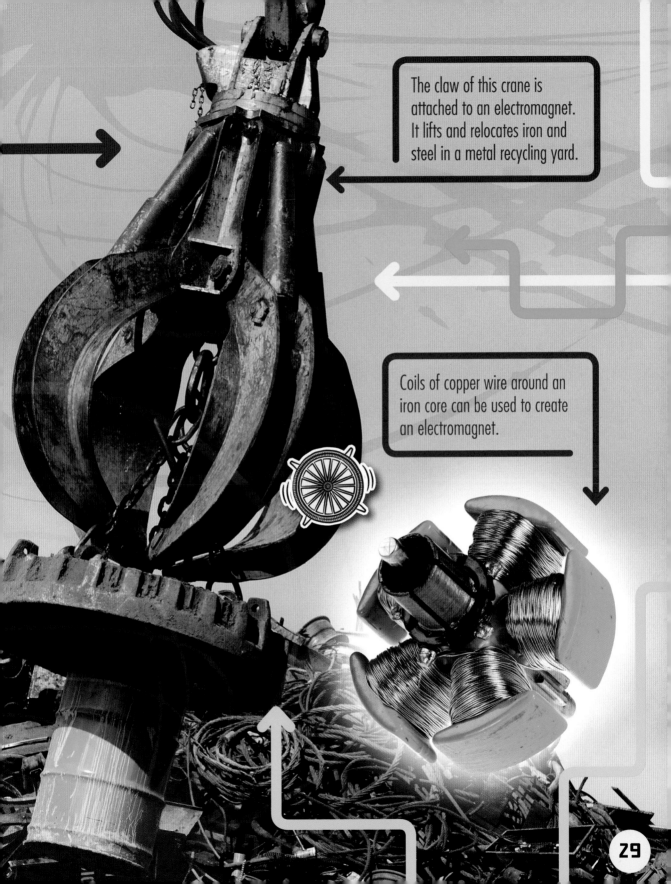

The claw of this crane is attached to an electromagnet. It lifts and relocates iron and steel in a metal recycling yard.

Coils of copper wire around an iron core can be used to create an electromagnet.

Generating electricity

It is not only possible to use electricity to make magnetism. We can also use magnets to make electricity. Electricity is the flow of electrical power from atoms. Currents of electricity are created when electrons are forced to move from atom to atom. As we have seen, magnets work by generating a magnetic field that pulls and pushes electrons within the atoms of objects near them, making the electrons move. Certain metals, such as copper, have electrons that are moved easily from their orbits. By moving a magnet quickly through a coil of copper wire, the changing magnetic field makes electrons flow in the wire. Electricity is created in this **generator**, and the movement of power is called an electric current.

Electricity is made in giant power plants like this one, and then carried to buildings through wires.

Transmission lines carrying electricity from power plants are held safely above the ground by huge towers called electricity pylons.

The electricity we use to power computers, lights and other appliances is produced in giant power plants. Most power plants burn large amounts of coal or other **fossil fuel** to boil water and produce steam. The steam is funnelled towards a big fan-like machine called a turbine, causing the turbine blades to spin. The spinning turbine rotates a coil of wire inside a magnetic field or spins a large, very powerful magnet inside a long coil of wire. This creates strong pulling and pushing forces in the coil of wire, which makes electrons in the wire move between atoms. An electric current flows through the wire.

Get smart!

Magnetism is used to control the strength of the electricity that flows to our homes. The electricity that travels out of power plants along metal cables is very powerful. Before it reaches our homes it passes through a **transformer** station. There, electrons pass through large coils that create magnetic fields which reduce the electricity's power, so that it is at a safe strength to use in our homes.

Get flowchart smart!

Electromagnetism makes electricity

Discover how magnets are used to produce electricity in power plants, following the flowchart.

Coal, gas or oil is burnt to provide heat.

Heat from the burning fuel is used to boil water in a boiler.

boiler

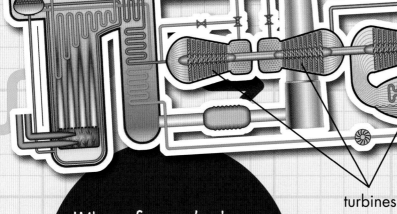

turbines

When free electrons are all moving in the same direction, an electric current is created.

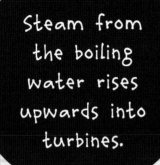

Steam from the boiling water rises upwards into turbines.

→

The steam turns the blades of the turbines.

The movement of the turbines moves a powerful magnet in a large coil of wire.

This creates a magnetic field that makes electrons break free from their atoms.

Flowchart Smart

Chapter 5

Magnets and motors

When you reach for an electric toothbrush, dry your hair with a hairdryer or cool yourself with an electric fan, you are enjoying the benefits of electromagnetism. One of the most important uses of electromagnetism is to power the electric motors that are in the machines we use every day.

An electric motor is a machine that uses energy from an electrical source, such as a battery or a socket, and changes that energy into movement energy to do some type of work. Motors are used in an incredible variety of machines, from computer hard drives and DVD players to ceiling fans and refrigerators.

When an electromagnet is used to make something spin or move, this movement can be used to make other parts of a machine spin, too. This is why motors can be used to drive moving parts in machines such as food mixers, drills and washing machines. For example, in an electric toothbrush, an electric motor spins the metal at the top of the device, and therefore the brush head we attach to that metal to clean and polish our teeth. In a vacuum cleaner, the motor turns the blades of a fan that sucks in dust and dirt from carpets.

Electromagnets create the motion in the head of your electric toothbrush, which loosens debris left behind in your teeth.

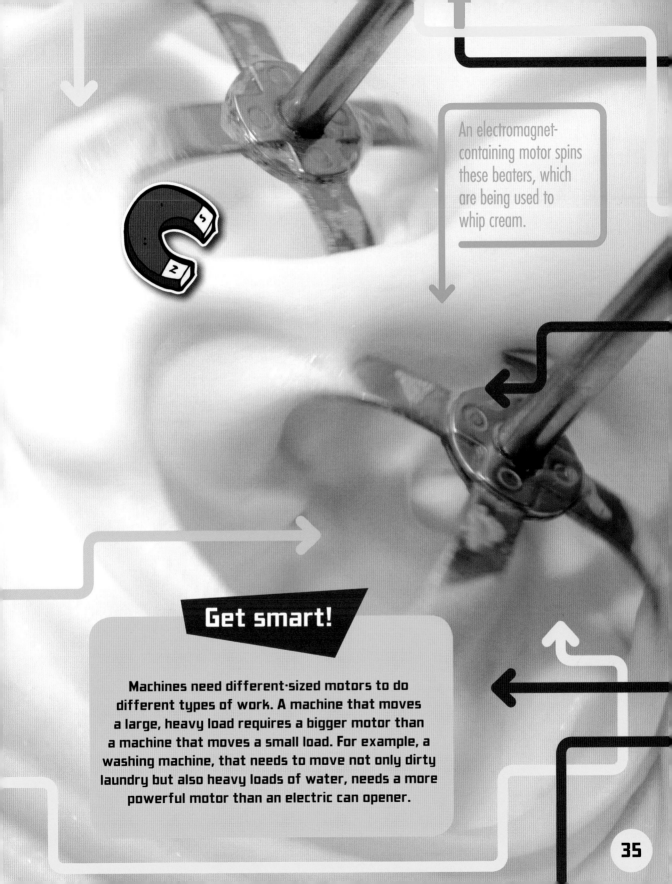

An electromagnet-containing motor spins these beaters, which are being used to whip cream.

Get smart!

Machines need different-sized motors to do different types of work. A machine that moves a large, heavy load requires a bigger motor than a machine that moves a small load. For example, a washing machine, that needs to move not only dirty laundry but also heavy loads of water, needs a more powerful motor than an electric can opener.

The key to grasping how an electric motor works is to understand how electromagnets can be controlled. One thing that makes electromagnets so incredibly useful is that we can change the amount of electricity that flows through them. The other clever thing about electromagnets is that we can also change the direction in which electricity flows through them. When we continually change the direction in which electricity flows through an electromagnet, we can make a motor work.

In a very simple motor, a movable loop of wire is positioned near a fixed magnet. When an electric current is passed through the wire, it becomes an electromagnet. When the south pole of the electromagnet is near the south pole of the fixed magnet, the like magnetic poles repel each other. The fixed magnet cannot move, so the electromagnet moves in the motor: its south pole moves away from the south pole of the fixed magnet. As it rotates, the south pole of the electromagnet gets nearer to the north pole of the fixed magnet and is pulled towards it because opposite magnetic poles attract each other.

Electromagnets make motors work in a huge variety of machines, including fun gadgets like this remote-controlled helicopter.

Just at the point at which the two opposite poles meet, a part called a **commutator** changes the direction in which the electricity is moving. When the direction of the electric current changes, the north and south poles of the electromagnet change places, too. Suddenly, the south pole of the electromagnet is near a south pole in the fixed magnet again, rather than a north pole. So the electromagnet continues to rotate as the two like poles repel each other and the two unlike poles attract each other. This happens again and again, at every half-turn of the electromagnet. This movement rotates other parts to which it is connected and causes them to move and spin and make the machine work.

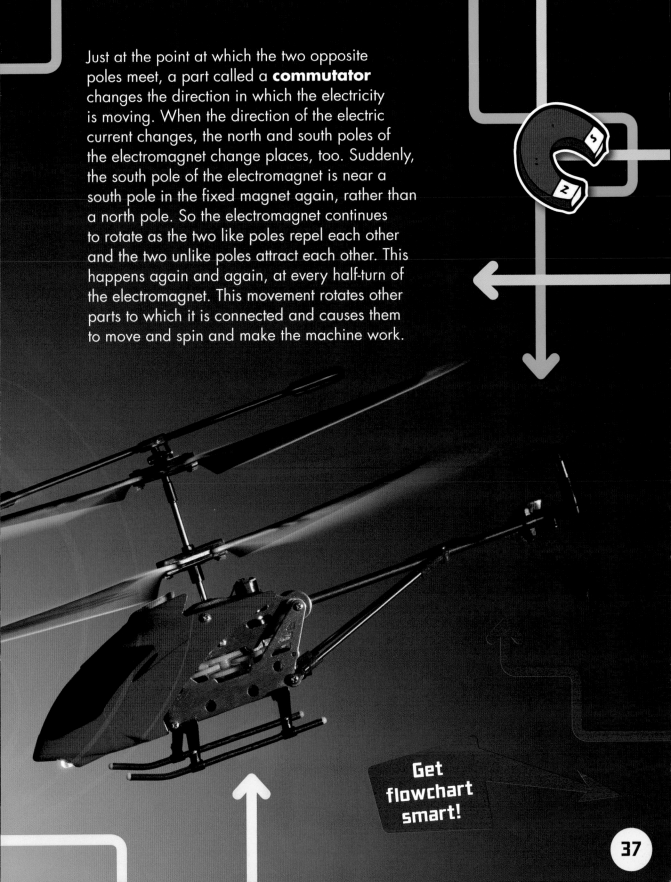

Get flowchart smart!

Electric motors

Follow the flowchart for a closer look at how electric motors work.

An electric current flows through a coil of wire that is free to rotate between two opposite magnetic poles.

Every half-turn, the direction of the electric current is changed to keep the coil of wire moving continuously in the same direction.

The coil of wire becomes an electromagnet. When its south pole faces the south pole of the magnet around it, the magnets repel each other. This magnetic force makes the coil of wire move.

When the south pole of the coil of wire faces the north pole of the magnet, the direction of the current is reversed.

This means two south poles are facing each other again, and again the magnetic force makes the coil of wire move.

Flowchart Smart

Chapter 6

Magnetism and us

Magnetism is an invisible force, but it is incredibly useful and it works for us in many different ways. It helps us power machines, navigate, travel and even detect illness.

In just one car, there are many magnets at work. Car GPS systems require magnetism to work, and there are magnets in the motors that move the windows up and down, work the windscreen wipers, adjust seats and mirrors, and start the engine. When you turn on the radio or put in a CD, magnets help you to hear music, too. As pulses of electricity travel through an electromagnet in a loudspeaker, the electromagnet is attracted to and repelled by a permanent magnet. It pushes and pulls a speaker cone, making it vibrate and produce sound waves that you can hear.

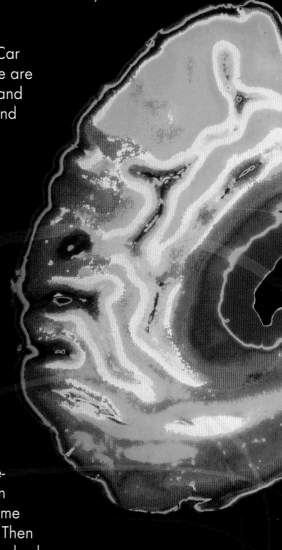

A magnetic resonance imaging (MRI) scanner is a machine that can make detailed images of the soft parts inside the human body. The human body is mostly water, and water consists of hydrogen and oxygen atoms. The protons in hydrogen atoms are like tiny magnets and are very sensitive to magnetic fields. When a patient lies in the MRI scanner, they are surrounded by a large, tube-shaped electromagnet, which causes the protons in the body to line up in the same direction, in the same way that a magnet pulls the needle of a compass. Then the machine sends **radio waves** to the part of the body to be tested, which disturbs the protons. When this happens, a computer works out where the protons are and what tissue they are part of. It uses this information to create images of the inside of the patient's body to see if any damage or disease is present.

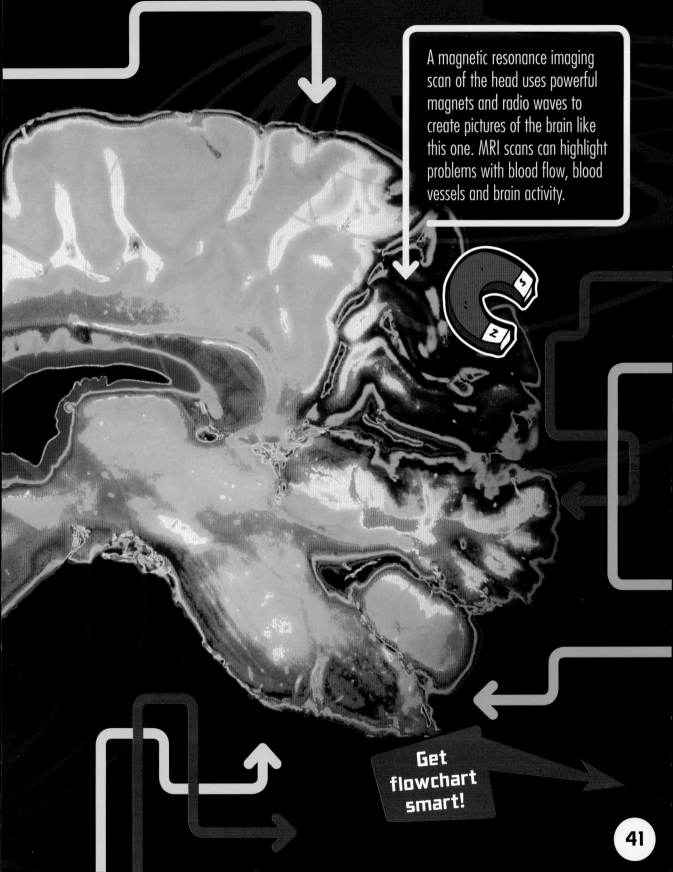

A magnetic resonance imaging scan of the head uses powerful magnets and radio waves to create pictures of the brain like this one. MRI scans can highlight problems with blood flow, blood vessels and brain activity.

Get flowchart smart!

How MRI
scanners work

Follow the flowchart for a closer look at MRI scanners.

A patient lies down inside an MRI scanner.

The scanner is switched on and an electromagnet creates a magnetic field.

Doctors use this information to work out whether there are any problems in body parts such as the brain, lungs or heart.

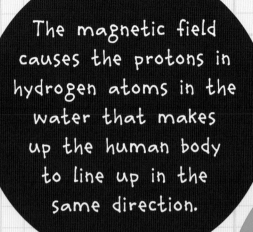

The magnetic field causes the protons in hydrogen atoms in the water that makes up the human body to line up in the same direction.

Radio waves disturb the protons and when they line up again they bounce back radio signals, which a computer picks up.

The computer can then work out where each atom is, and even what type of tissue it belongs to.

Magnetism in the future

Humans have been using magnetism since its discovery, and we are finding new ways to use its powers all the time. In the future, we could all be driving electric cars, and astronauts could be launched into space from a magnetic launchpad.

Electric cars do not look different to ordinary cars, but they are powered by an electric motor instead of a petrol engine. Electric cars produce fewer of the gases that become trapped in our atmosphere and contribute to climate change. More countries may also start to use maglev trains. These trains use magnetism to float, without friction, on top of a special track, resulting in a faster and more efficient method of transport. It is also possible that the magnetic technology used to make maglev trains may also be used to create magnetic ramps to launch rockets into space. This would save some of the vast amounts of fuel required to launch a spacecraft today.

Some scientists think magnets could be used to upset the electrical sensors that sharks use to navigate. It may eventually be possible to use this technology to move sharks away from a populated area.

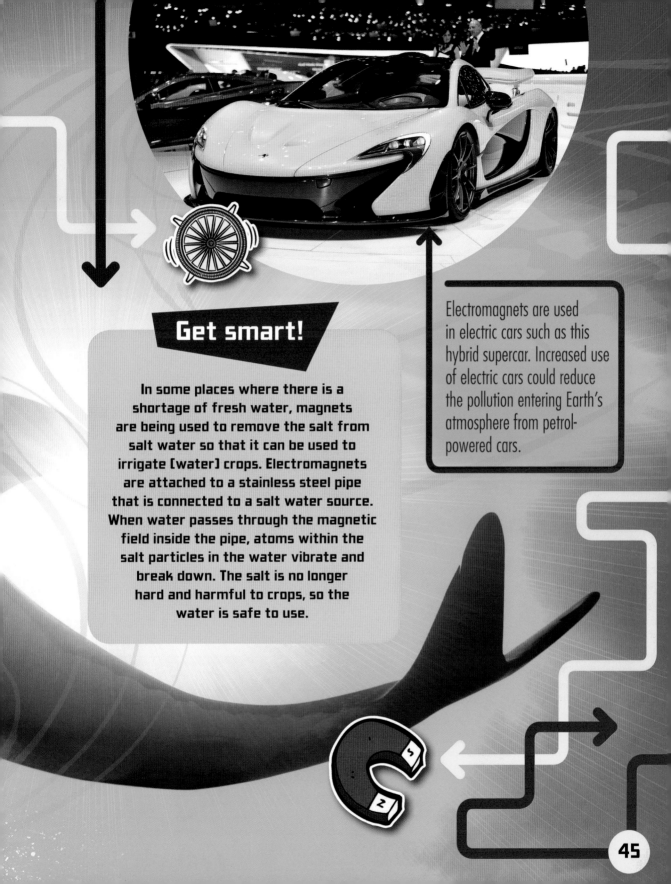

Electromagnets are used in electric cars such as this hybrid supercar. Increased use of electric cars could reduce the pollution entering Earth's atmosphere from petrol-powered cars.

Get smart!

In some places where there is a shortage of fresh water, magnets are being used to remove the salt from salt water so that it can be used to irrigate (water) crops. Electromagnets are attached to a stainless steel pipe that is connected to a salt water source. When water passes through the magnetic field inside the pipe, atoms within the salt particles in the water vibrate and break down. The salt is no longer hard and harmful to crops, so the water is safe to use.

Glossary

alloy substance made from a mixture of metals

atom smallest particle of a substance that can exist by itself

commutator device in an electrical machine that can reverse the direction of the electric current

compass device used to find directions, with magnetic needle that always points north

core centre

demagnetize take away the magnetism from a magnet

electric current steady flow of electrons

electromagnet magnet that becomes magnetic when electric currents pass through it

electron negatively charged particle that whirls around the nucleus of an atom

energy ability or power to do work

ferromagnetic attracted to magnets or that can be made into a permanent magnet; iron is a ferromagnetic material

fossil fuel fuel formed from the remains of ancient living things; fossil fuels include oil, coal or gas

generator machine that creates electricity by turning a magnet inside a coil of wire

keeper iron bar placed across the ends of a magnet to stop it from losing its magnetism

magnet material that causes invisible pulling or pushing forces

magnetic field area near a magnetic object in which magnetic forces can be detected

motor device that produces power to make machines work

navigate follow a course to get from one place to another

neutron particle in the nucleus of an atom that has no electric charge

nucleus centre of an atom

orbit follow a circular path around an object

permanent magnet magnet that attracts magnetic materials with the same strength until it is damaged

pivot point on which something turns

pole one of two points, north and south, at opposite ends of a magnet or at the opposite ends of Earth

proton positively charged particle in an atom's nucleus that does not move

radio wave electromagnetic wave used to carry signals through the air

resistance measure of how well an object restricts the flow of current or magnetism

temporary magnet magnet made from materials that are easy to magnetize but lose their magnetism quickly and easily

transformer device that increases or decreases voltage of an electric current

Find out more

Books

Machines and Motors (Infographic How It Works), Jon Richards (Wayland, 2016)

Magnets and Springs (How Does Science Work?), Carol Ballard (Wayland, 2014)

Speedy Science, Angela Royston (Franklin Watts, 2014)

Utterly Amazing Science, Robert Winston (Dorling Kindersley, 2014)

Websites

Check out this news clip about how magnets are changing the way we travel:
www.bbc.co.uk/newsround/36324803

Watch how magnets are used in a scrapyard:
www.bbc.co.uk/education/clips/zcntsbk

Discover more about magnets at:
www.dkfindout.com/uk/search/magnets

Index

48